Vol 4

MAZE

Ages 4-6

FOR KIDS

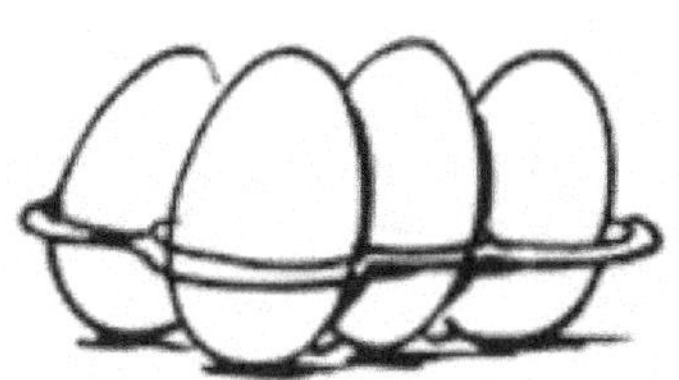

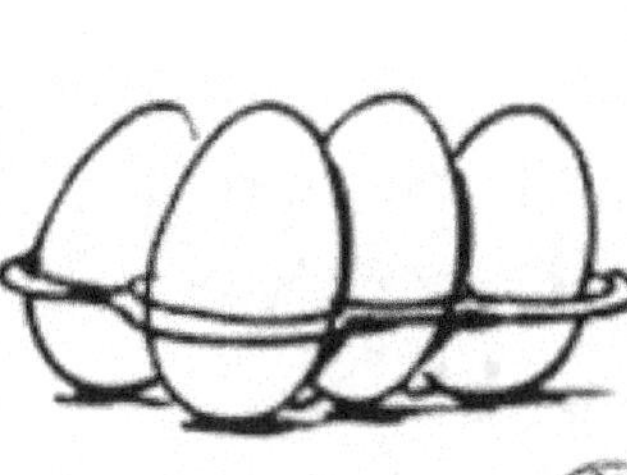

MAZE BOOK

SOCIAL MEDIA

- /MySweetBooks1
- /MySweetBooks1
- /MySweetBooks1
- /MySweetBooks

Email Us : mysweetbooks1@gmail.com

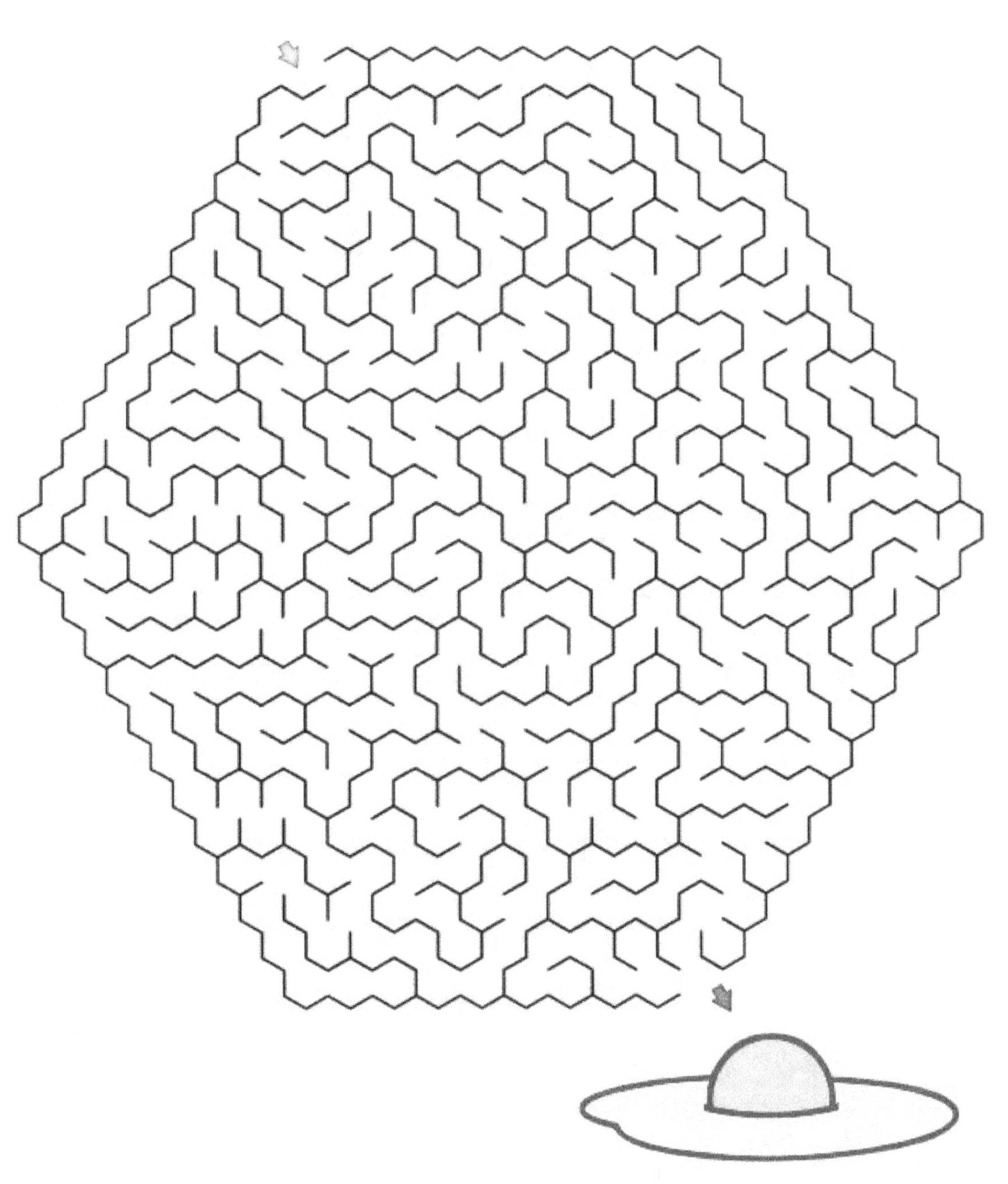

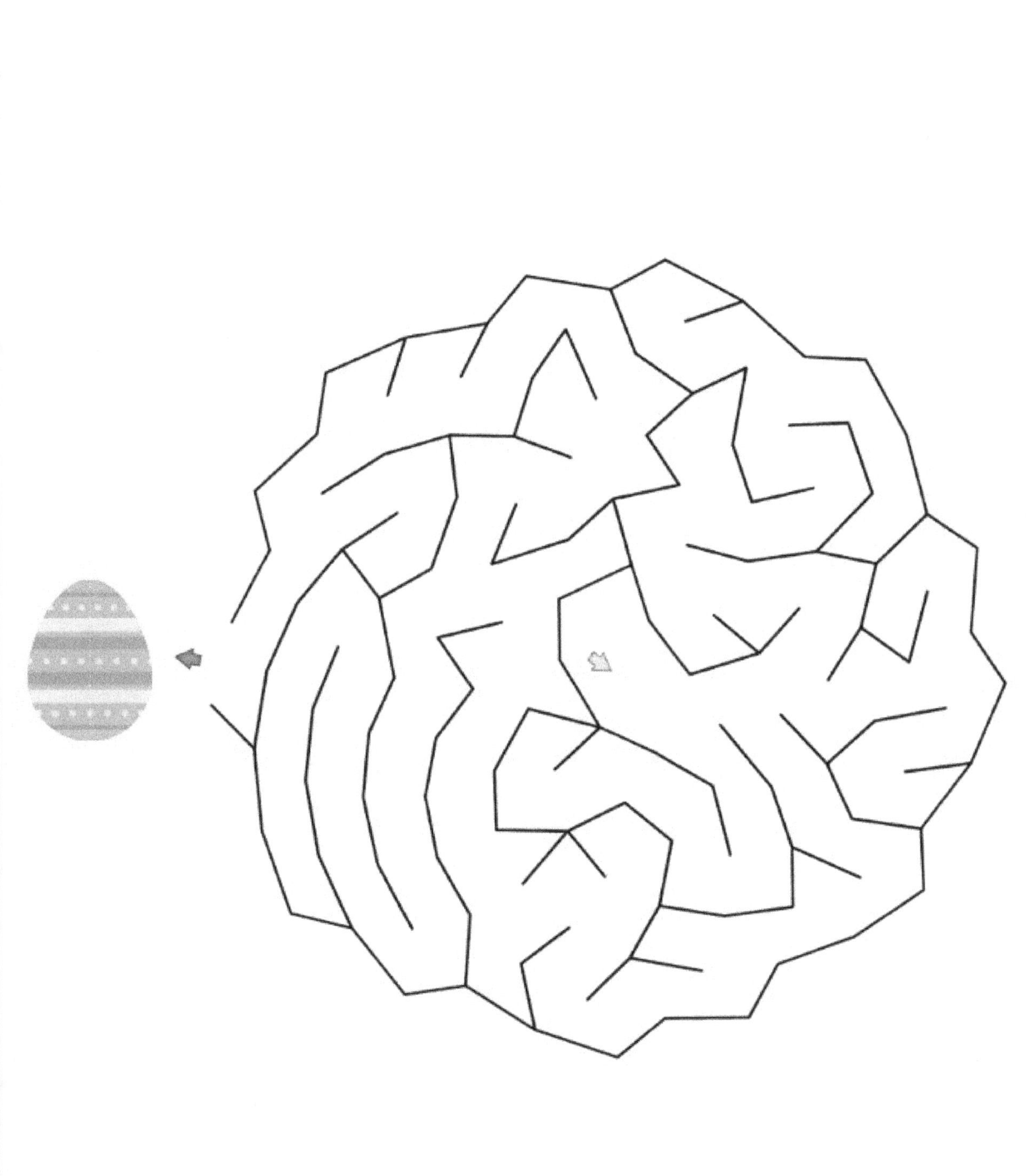

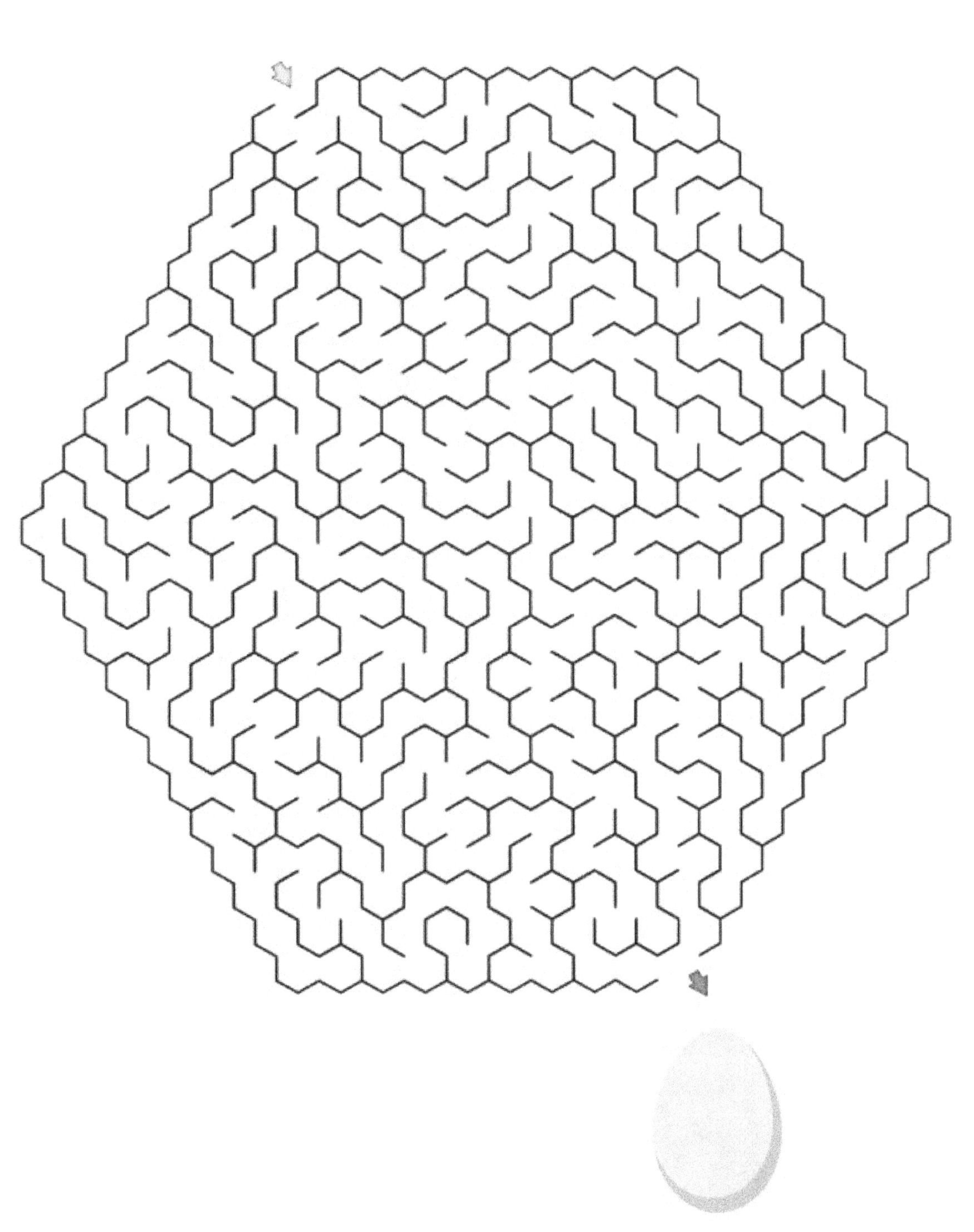

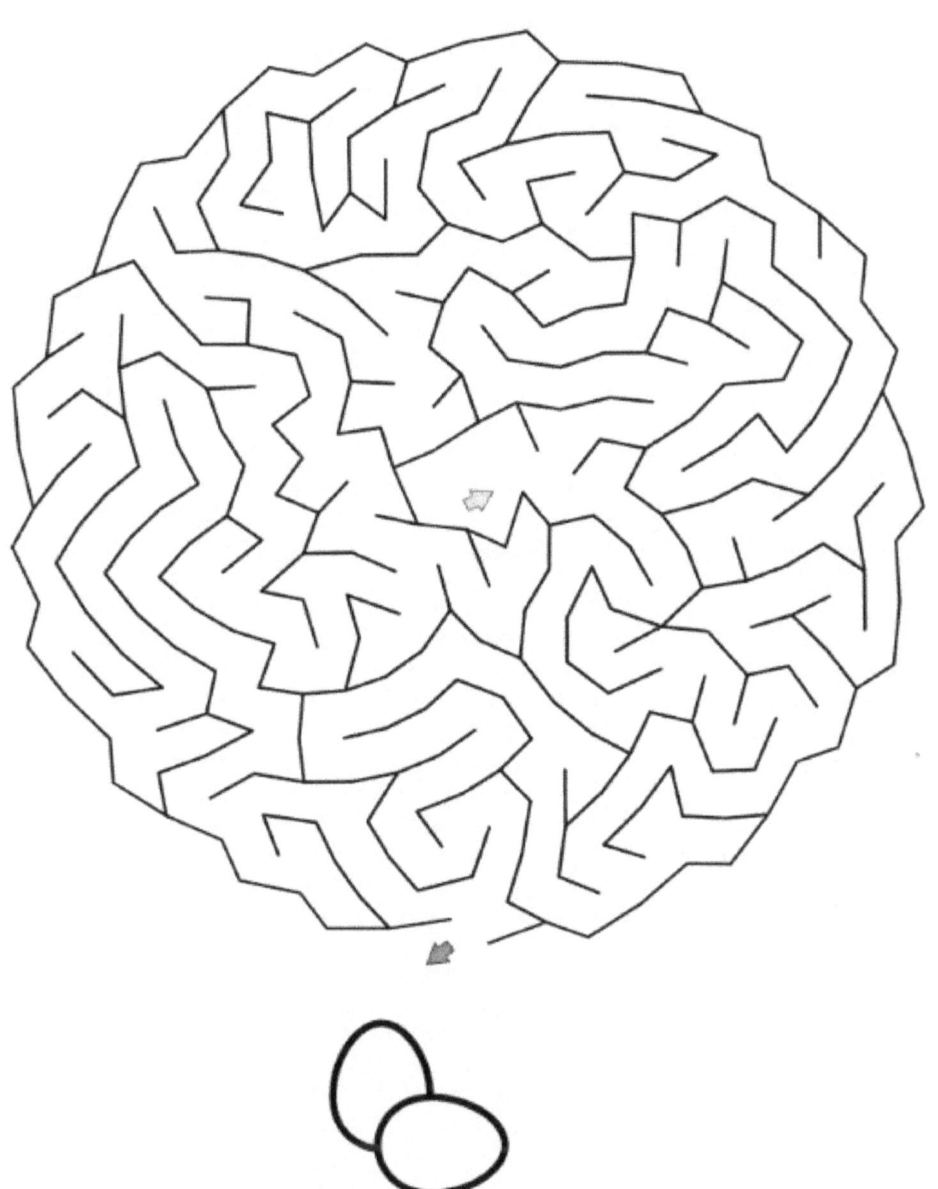

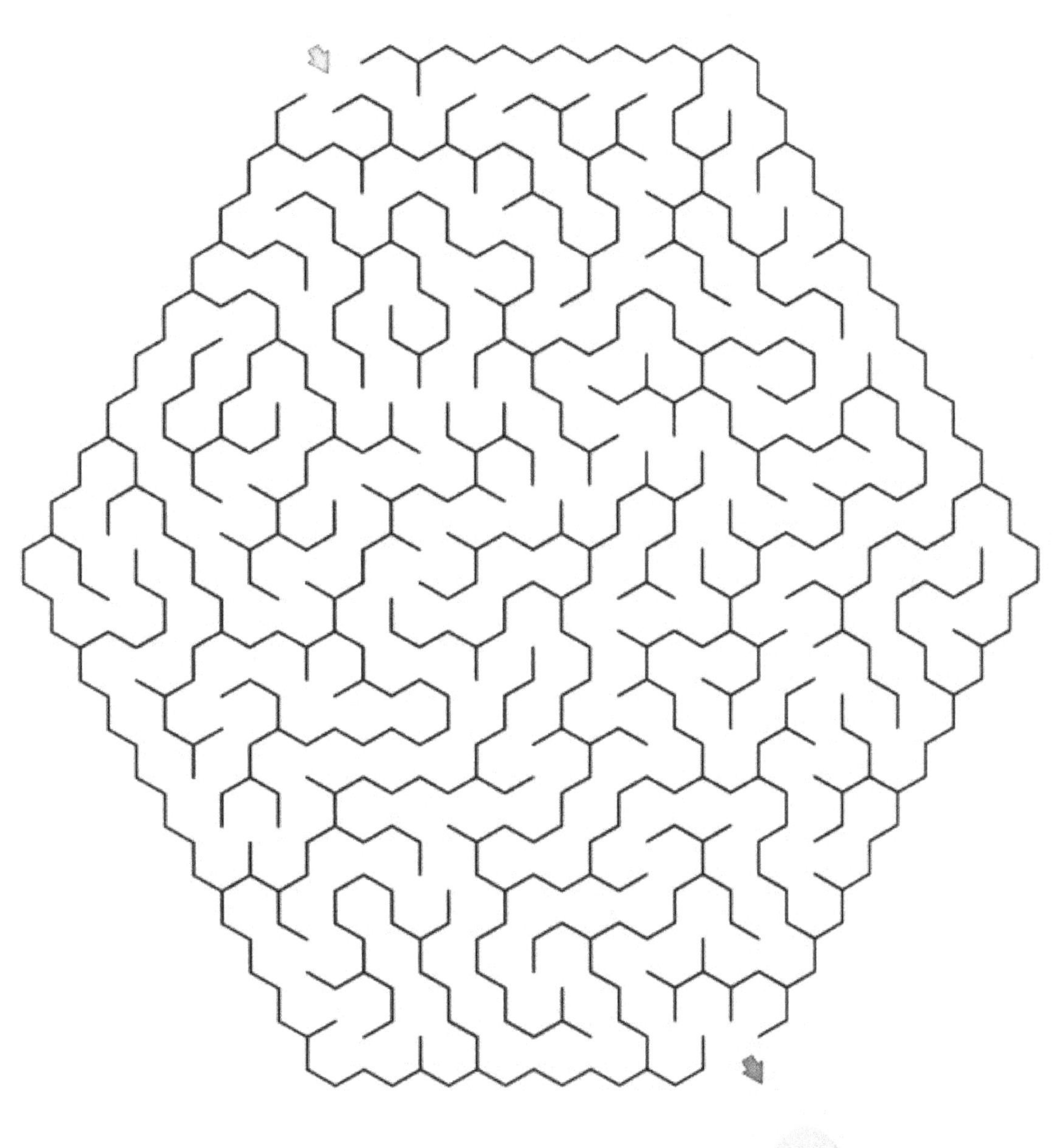

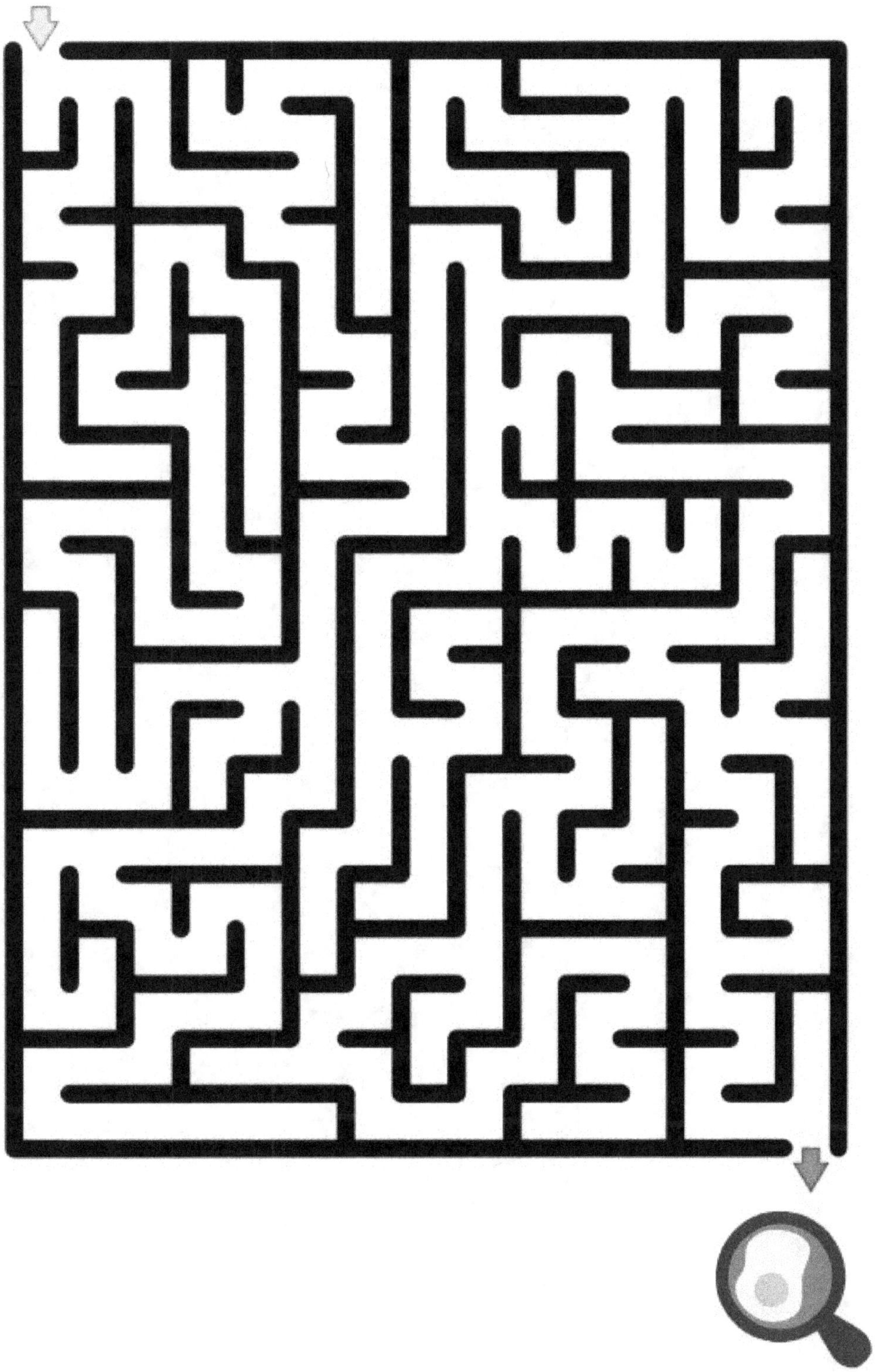

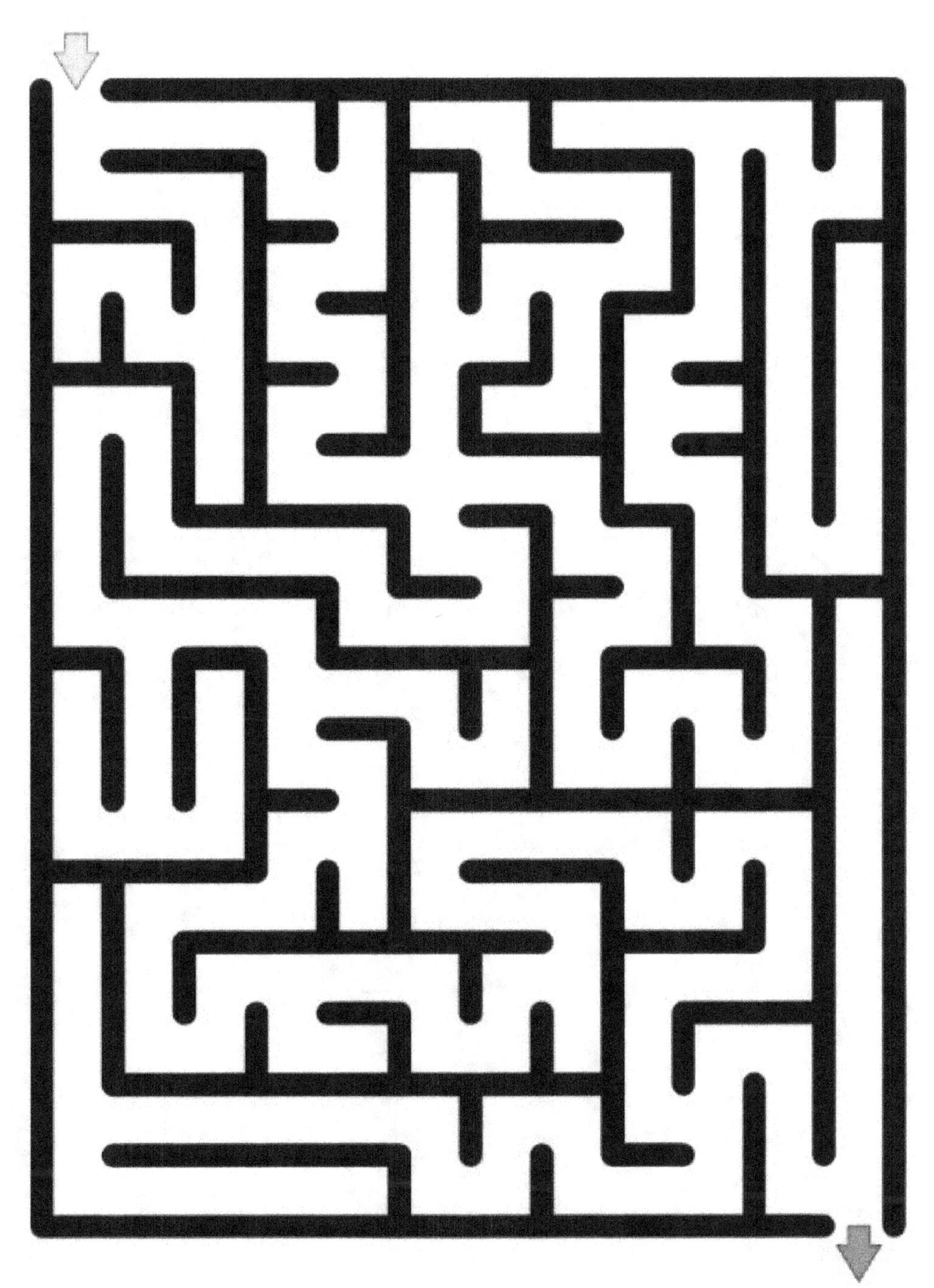

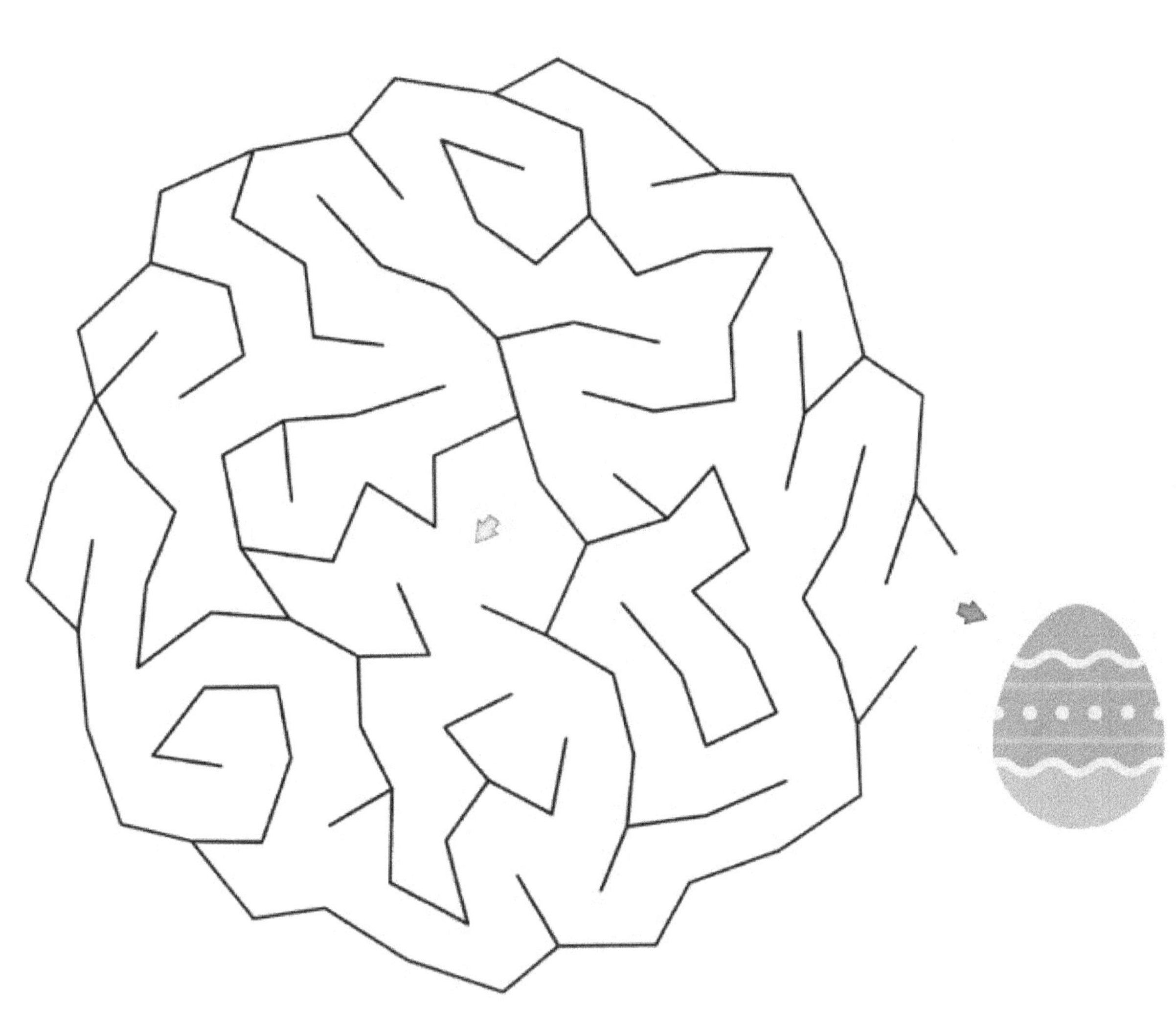

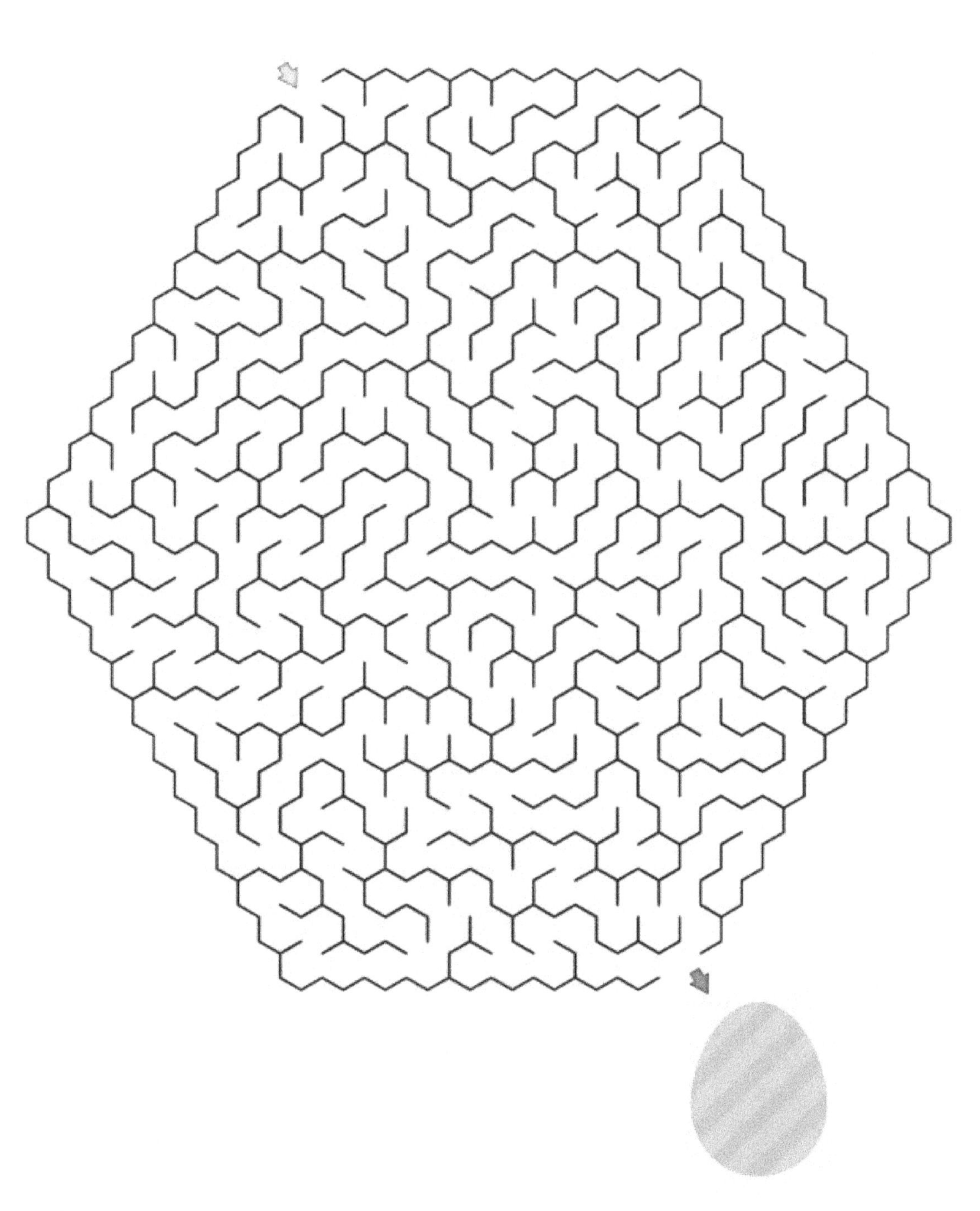

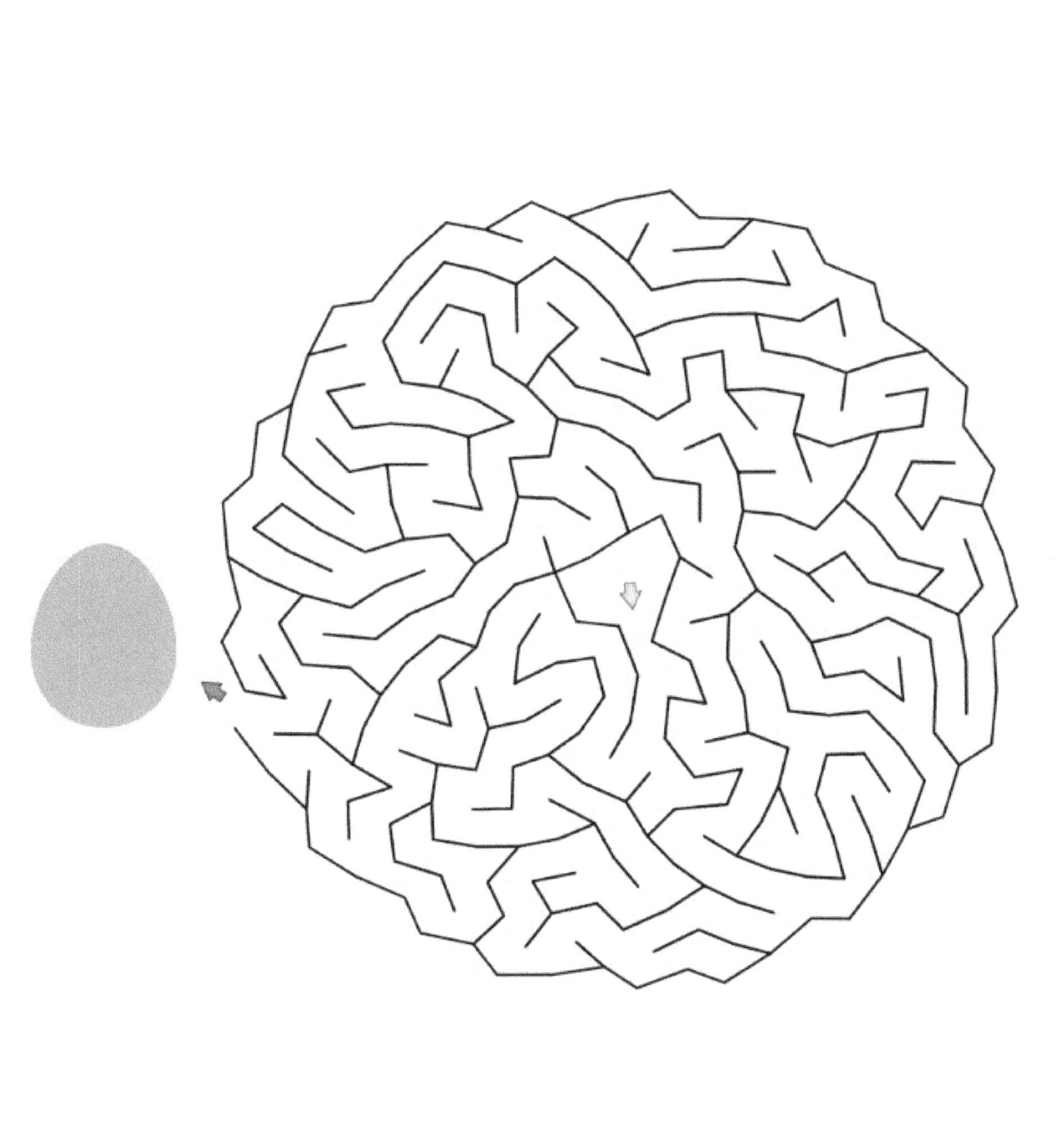

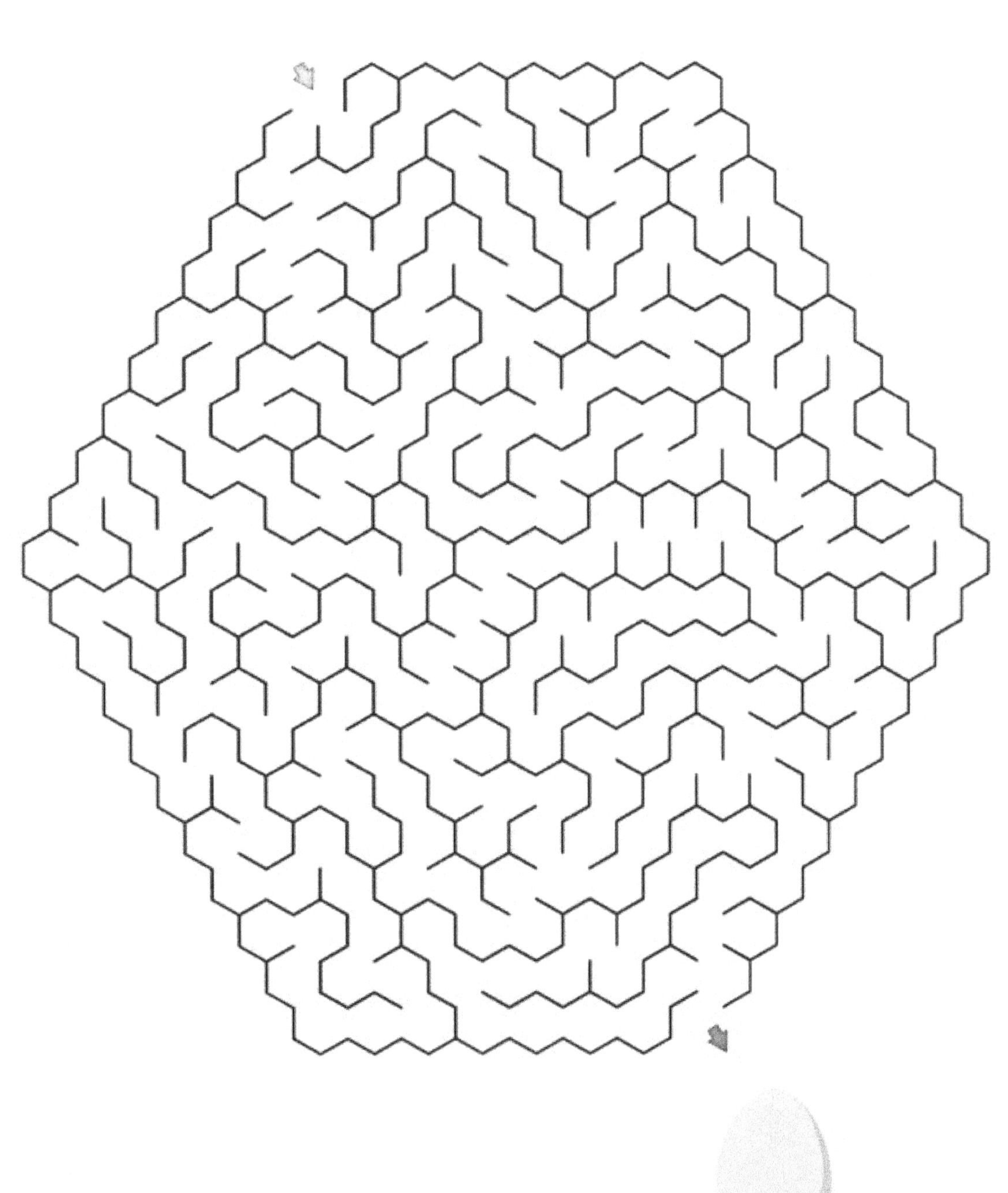

www.ingramcontent.com/pod-product-compliance
Lightning Source LLC
Chambersburg PA
CBHW081736250726
48657CB00010B/3301